Anthony
Wayne

American General

Colonial Leaders

Lord Baltimore
English Politician and Colonist

Benjamin Banneker
American Mathematician and Astronomer

Sir William Berkeley
Governor of Virginia

William Bradford
Governor of Plymouth Colony

Jonathan Edwards
Colonial Religious Leader

Benjamin Franklin
American Statesman, Scientist, and Writer

Anne Hutchinson
Religious Leader

Cotton Mather
Author, Clergyman, and Scholar

Increase Mather
Clergyman and Scholar

James Oglethorpe
Humanitarian and Soldier

William Penn
Founder of Democracy

Sir Walter Raleigh
English Explorer and Author

Caesar Rodney
American Patriot

John Smith
English Explorer and Colonist

Miles Standish
Plymouth Colony Leader

Peter Stuyvesant
Dutch Military Leader

George Whitefield
Clergyman and Scholar

Roger Williams
Founder of Rhode Island

John Winthrop
Politician and Statesman

John Peter Zenger
Free Press Advocate

Revolutionary War Leaders

John Adams
Second U.S. President

Samuel Adams
Patriot

Ethan Allen
Revolutionary Hero

Benedict Arnold
Traitor to the Cause

John Burgoyne
British General

George Rogers Clark
American General

Lord Cornwallis
British General

Thomas Gage
British General

King George III
English Monarch

Nathanael Greene
Military Leader

Nathan Hale
Revolutionary Hero

Alexander Hamilton
First U.S. Secretary of the Treasury

John Hancock
President of the Continental Congress

Patrick Henry
American Statesman and Speaker

William Howe
British General

John Jay
First Chief Justice of the Supreme Court

Thomas Jefferson
Author of the Declaration of Independence

John Paul Jones
Father of the U.S. Navy

Thaddeus Kosciuszko
Polish General and Patriot

Lafayette
French Freedom Fighter

James Madison
Father of the Constitution

Francis Marion
The Swamp Fox

James Monroe
American Statesman

Thomas Paine
Political Writer

Molly Pitcher
Heroine

Paul Revere
American Patriot

Betsy Ross
American Patriot

Baron Von Steuben
American General

George Washington
First U.S. President

Anthony Wayne
American General

Famous Figures of the Civil War Era

John Brown
Abolitionist

Jefferson Davis
Confederate President

Frederick Douglass
Abolitionist and Author

Stephen A. Douglas
Champion of the Union

David Farragut
Union Admiral

Ulysses S. Grant
Military Leader and President

Stonewall Jackson
Confederate General

Joseph E. Johnston
Confederate General

Robert E. Lee
Confederate General

Abraham Lincoln
Civil War President

George Gordon Meade
Union General

George McClellan
Union General

William Henry Seward
Senator and Statesman

Philip Sheridan
Union General

William Sherman
Union General

Edwin Stanton
Secretary of War

Harriet Beecher Stowe
Author of Uncle Tom's Cabin

James Ewell Brown Stuart
Confederate General

Sojourner Truth
Abolitionist, Suffragist, and Preacher

Harriet Tubman
Leader of the Underground Railroad

Anthony Wayne

American General

Patricia Grabowski

Arthur M. Schlesinger, jr.
Senior Consulting Editor

Chelsea House Publishers

Philadelphia

CHELSEA HOUSE PUBLISHERS
Editor-in-Chief Sally Cheney
Director of Production Kim Shinners
Production Manager Pamela Loos
Art Director Sara Davis
Production Editor Diann Grasse

Staff for *ANTHONY WAYNE*
Editor Sally Cheney
Associate Art Director Takeshi Takahashi
Series Design Keith Trego
Cover Design 21st Century Publishing and Communications, Inc.
Picture Researcher Pat Holl
Layout 21st Century Publishing and Communications, Inc.

The Chelsea House World Wide Web address is
http://www.chelseahouse.com

First Printing
1 3 5 7 9 8 6 4 2

Library of Congress Cataloging-in-Publication Data

Grabowski, Patricia A.
    General "Mad" Anthony Wayne / Patricia Grabowski.
        p. cm. — (Revolutionary War leaders)
    Includes bibliographical references and index.
    ISBN 0-7910-6382-8 (hc : alk. paper) — ISBN 0-7910-6383-6
    (pbk. : alk. paper)
        1. Wayne, Anthony, 1745-1796—Juvenile literature. 2. Generals
    —United States—Biography—Juvenile literature. 3. United States.
    Continental Army—Biography—Juvenile literature. 4. United
    States—History—Revolution, 1775-1783—Campaigns—Juvenile
    literature. [1. Wayne, Anthony, 1745-1796. 2. Generals. 3. United
    States. Continental Army. 4. United States—History—Revolution,
    1775-1783.] I. Title. II. Series.

E207.W35 G7 2001
977.3'092—dc21
[B]   2001028518

Publisher's Note: In Colonial and Revolutionary War America, there were no standard rules for spelling, punctuation, capitalization, or grammar. Some of the quotations that appear in the Colonial Leaders and Revolutionary War Leaders series come from original documents and letters written during this time in history. Original quotations reflect writing inconsistencies of the period.

Contents

Anthony Wayne's grandfather had the family estate built on
386 acres of land close to the village of Paoli, which is located
near Philadelphia. Anthony's father inherited the estate in 1739
and named it Waynesborough.

Life at Waynesborough

In 1722, Captain Anthony Wayne sailed from England to America. His wife, Hannah, and eight of their nine children were with him. Their son Isaac remained in England to finish his education, and he arrived in America two years later.

Captain Wayne was born in Ireland and joined the British army as a young man. He became known as a hero after leading his troops to victory in the Battle of the Boyne in Ireland. Retired from the army, he was about to start an exciting adventure in the New World.

The Wayne family first landed in Boston, and later they traveled south to Chester County, Pennsylvania. Captain Wayne bought 386 acres of land there and he built a large home near the village of Paoli. Captain Wayne died in 1739 and was buried in the churchyard of St. David's in Radnor. His son, Isaac, inherited the estate and built an addition to the house. He named the estate Waynesborough.

The large, two-storied house was built of brown stone. At the entrance, there was a heavy door. It consisted of two layers of wooden boards with a sheet of iron sandwiched between them. Captain Wayne had wanted it to be strong to keep the house safe from Indian attacks.

Isaac and Elizabeth Iddings Wayne raised their family at Waynesborough. They had four children. Their first son, William, died soon after he was born. Anthony was born on January 1, 1745. Hannah was born when

Anthony was three years old and Ann, the youngest child, arrived in 1751.

Anthony was a strong, healthy baby. When his parents named him after his famous grandfather, they couldn't have guessed that he would become a military hero as well. Anthony's daring deeds during the American Revolution would make him even more famous than Captain Wayne.

Grandfather Wayne had been right to worry about Indian attacks. When Anthony was a little boy, the French and Indian War began. The French wanted to force the British out of the Ohio country, as the area was called, and claim it as their own. In 1752, a group of French soldiers attacked Picawillany, a British trading post in Ohio. The Indians, who were **allies** with the French, agreed to help them fight the British.

At the time, Pennsylvania was a British colony. Isaac Wayne was worried because

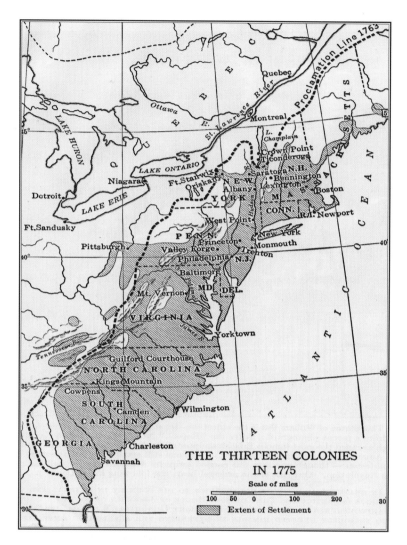

THE THIRTEEN COLONIES
IN 1775

Scale of miles

100 50 0   100   200

Extent of Settlement

This map shows Great Britain's 13 colonies as they looked in 1775.

Indians commanded by the French had crossed the Allegheny Mountains. They had attacked settlers within 60 miles of the city of Philadelphia. Isaac joined the militia to help defend his family and neighbors.

The fighting lasted for two years. With the help of colonists like Isaac Wayne, the British finally defeated the French and their Indian allies. After the war, Isaac was elected to the Colonial Assembly and served as a member from 1757 to 1764.

Anthony was greatly influenced by all that he saw and heard about the war. He watched as soldiers returned from the fighting, and listened to their stories. He looked forward to his father's occasional visit and begged Isaac for stories about the war.

Anthony went to school in Easttown, Pennsylvania, at a school run by his uncle, Gilbert Wayne. But he was not a good student. He was more interested in playing war games than in studying his lessons.

One day at school, Anthony and his classmates acted out the July 1758 capture of Fort Ticonderoga. The boys played bravely, unconcerned with their bruises, black eyes, and bloody noses. Their parents complained, though, and Uncle Gilbert decided to do something about Anthony's bad behavior.

Gilbert wrote a letter to Anthony's father, saying, "One thing I am certain of, he will never make a **scholar;** he may perhaps make a soldier. . . . I must be candid with you, brother Isaac–unless Anthony pays more attention to his books, I shall be under the painful necessity of dismissing him from the school."

After reading the letter, Isaac Wayne spoke to his son and helped him understand that schoolwork was very important. From then on, Anthony worked very hard in school. He did especially well in mathematics and made his father proud.

A year and a half later, Uncle Gilbert again wrote to his brother. But this time, he praised Anthony for his hard work. Gilbert said there was nothing more he could teach

Anthony Wayne lived and studied at the Academy of Philadelphia. He was a handsome and popular young man who often attended parties with wealthy Philadelphians.

Anthony. He suggested that Isaac send Anthony to the Academy of Philadelphia to continue his education.

Isaac took his son to Philadelphia and enrolled Anthony in the academy. He bought him new clothes and rented a room in which Anthony would stay. Anthony studied at the academy for two years, where he learned how to be a surveyor. He also attended many parties and was popular with the wealthy residents of the city. Anthony was handsome and was considered to be a gentleman. In fact, because of his good looks and fine clothes, he was often called a "dandy." A dandy was a well-dressed gentleman, usually with good manners.

After leaving the academy, Anthony spent time exploring the Pennsylvania wilderness. He also studied civil engineering and astronomy. Then he opened a small surveyor's office in Philadelphia and did jobs for local citizens. Around the same time, colonial leader Benjamin Franklin, along with some other men, entered into a business deal. They purchased 200,000 acres of land along the St. John's and Piticoodzack Rivers in Nova Scotia, Canada.

They wanted to establish a settlement there. Franklin asked John Hughes, one of his partners in the project, to find someone to survey the land and take charge of the settlement. Hughes offered the job to Anthony Wayne. This was a wonderful opportunity for a young man who was only 20 years old.

Anthony took his job very seriously. He surveyed the borders of the land, and selected places where mills and ferries would be placed. Anthony mapped out roads, mountains, islands, swamps, and forests. When the settlers came, he helped them choose their land and build their homes.

Anthony was very good at his job, and Hughes was pleased with his accomplishments. But trouble was brewing between England and its colonies. After two years, the settlement was closed. The owners refused to send any more settlers, and Anthony returned home.

While he was at school, Anthony met Mary Penrose. Their families had known each other for a long time. Anthony began calling on Mary and visited her as often as he could. He wanted to ask her to marry him. But before he could do so, he had to show her family that he had a good job. By the time Anthony returned from Nova Scotia, he had gained respect and a good reputation for his work. This pleased Mary's parents, and on March 25, 1766, Anthony and Mary were married. The young couple went to live at Waynesborough.

For the next few years, Anthony ran the family farm and operated his own successful tannery. The tannery treated animal hides and made them into leather. Anthony continued his surveying work as well. The Waynes' two children, Margaretta and Isaac, were born during this time—Margaretta in 1768 and Isaac in 1772.

In 1774, Anthony's father died and he

inherited Waynesborough and all of his father's wealth. His friends and neighbors looked up to him as a respected leader of the colony.

Colonists protested against England's high taxes on tea coming into America. While dressed as Native Americans, colonists threw a shipment of tea into Boston Harbor at what became known as the Boston Tea Party.

A Young Soldier

The British fought against the French for control of land in the French and Indian War, also known as the Seven Years' War. The Paris peace treaty ended the fighting in 1763. England had spent a lot of money during the war years, and the country's treasury was nearly empty. Since the French and Indian War was fought on American soil, the British government thought the colonists should help pay for it.

In 1765, Parliament passed the Stamp Act, which placed a tax on newspapers and legal documents. Colonists protested so much, it was removed the following year. Then England placed a tax on goods coming into the colonies. Tea was one of the items that was taxed heavily. On December 16, 1773, a group of colonists dressed as Native Americans boarded a ship docked in Boston Harbor. They dumped the entire shipment of tea into the water to protest the tax. This incident became known as the Boston Tea Party.

In September 1774 the First Continental Congress met in Philadelphia. Twelve of the thirteen colonies sent representatives. As a result of this meeting, the colonists decided that Parliament had no right to impose taxes or enforce certain laws in the colonies.

News of these events soon reached the citizens of Pennsylvania. In October 1774, Anthony was

Boston wasn't the only city to host a tea party. In October 1773, colonists learned that a ship named *The Polly* was headed to Philadelphia. On December 25, when the ship arrived, the citizens were outraged. They held a meeting. Colonial leaders told Captain Ayers that it would be dangerous for him to unload the tea. Ayers understood their threat to destroy the shipment. He was permitted to stay in Philadelphia overnight to get supplies for his return to England, but he left the next day without unloading his ship.

elected to the Chester County Committee of Safety and to the Provincial Assembly of Pennsylvania. He started to believe that war was unavoidable. In preparation, he began to study books about war and military science.

On April 19, 1775, the first shots of the American Revolution were fired at the towns of Lexington and Concord in Massachusetts. In May the Second Continental Congress **convened**. This time each of the colonies sent delegates to Philadelphia. Anthony was asked to represent Pennsylvania. Most of the assemblymen were opposed to breaking away from England. They still hoped the matter could be settled peacefully. But Anthony believed in standing up for his rights and those of his neighbors. He was strongly against the British actions.

A few days later, the Chester County Committee of Safety decided to form a **militia** and gather weapons and ammunition. Over the next few months, Anthony spent his time drilling the militia. He also helped organize a naval force. In August 1775 he helped write the rules and regulations for the Pennsylvania militia and navy.

In the meantime, the Second Continental Congress asked Pennsylvania to form four battalions of **infantry**. Anthony was unanimously chosen to lead one of the battalions. On January 3, 1776, he was commissioned a colonel and given command of the Fourth Battalion. He immediately began drilling and training his soldiers.

In February, Congress asked Anthony to speed up his preparations. He was ordered to join George Washington in New York as soon as possible. There had been some difficulty getting weapons for all the soldiers. Since he didn't want anyone to march unarmed, he sent only three companies to New York.

A few days later, Anthony headed north to Canada with three more companies. He was supposed to help General John Thomas with the siege of Quebec. By the time he got there, the

Shown here are examples of uniforms worn by the Continental Army. Starting at the left is the uniform of the Third Pennsylvania Regiment; Washington's Guard; Second Regiment, South Carolina Infantry; Eleventh Virginia Regiment; and Maryland Riflemen.

siege had failed, and the army was retreating.

In April, Washington sent General John Sullivan to Canada with six more battalions.

Anthony and three of his companies went with Sullivan. When they reached Sorel, a village on Lake Champlain, they learned that a small British force was stationed at Three Rivers. Colonel Arthur St. Clair took 600 men to capture the British post. General William Thompson and Colonel Wayne joined him. Instead of the small force they expected, the Americans found thousands of British soldiers just across the river.

General Thompson ordered his troops to cross the river. He split them into five divisions, with Anthony commanding one of the divisions. They were outnumbered by the British. After several hours of fighting, the Americans began to retreat. Anthony kept the British busy while the rest of the army escaped to New York. Before the end of the fight, he was left with only twenty soldiers and six officers. But Anthony was able to hold back the British army for an hour. He had fooled them into thinking that he had a larger force. Finally, Anthony and his men escaped into the woods. He received a leg wound in the action. Anthony's

Thomas Jefferson (standing) was asked by the Second Continental Congress to write the Declaration of Independence, which states that the colonies wanted to be free of England's rule.

brave deeds and cool head saved the Continental Army from being destroyed.

After the American defeat at the Battle of Three Rivers, Congress decided to take drastic action. They asked Thomas Jefferson, a young lawyer from Virginia, to write a letter. In it, he stated that the colonies no longer wanted to be ruled by England. They wanted to be free to form their own country. This letter was called the Declaration of Independence. It was signed on July 4, 1776, by representatives from the colonies.

In mid-July, the American army left Canada and went to Fort Ticonderoga in New York. Seven regiments from Ticonderoga marched south to join General George Washington, who had crossed the Delaware River to escape Britian's General Howe. The British Army under Commander Carleton stayed in Canada and settled down for the winter.

Anthony Wayne took command of Fort Ticonderoga on November 18, 1776. Living conditions there were terrible. The men needed everything from clothing to shoes. There was very little food and no medicine for the sick. As a result, many of the soldiers died from disease and starvation.

Another problem arose at the beginning of

1777. Some of the soldiers had agreed to serve for only one year. In February a group of men led by Captain Neilson prepared to leave. When Anthony questioned them, they told him that they had served their time. After some discussion, Anthony convinced them to stay.

On February 21, Congress promoted Anthony to the rank of brigadier general. His success in rescuing St. Clair's force at Three Rivers probably had something to do with this decision.

Anthony was bored at Fort Ticonderoga. He wanted to be back in action. In the early months of 1777, he asked to join General Washington. On April 12, his request was granted, and Anthony received orders to report to Washington in Morristown, New Jersey.

American soldiers are shown here on their march to Valley Forge. The journey was difficult due to snow and a lack of proper shoes and clothing.

3

The Road to Independence

When Anthony arrived in Morristown in May 1777, Washington's army consisted of five divisions. Anthony was given command of the division known as the Pennsylvania Line. He immediately began training his men. Many of them were new soldiers and didn't know anything about fighting a war.

On July 5, British troops commanded by General Burgoyne captured Fort Ticonderoga. British General Howe was preparing to march north from New York to join him. But Howe's plans changed when American General Charles Lee was taken prisoner.

Lee betrayed the Americans by offering Howe a plan to capture Philadelphia. Howe was excited by the idea of occupying Philadelphia, which was the American capital at that time. He left New York and arrived in Elk Ferry, near the Chesapeake Bay, on August 15.

In the meantime, George Washington marched his army through Philadelphia. They camped on the Red Clay Creek in Delaware. Anthony suggested a surprise attack. He believed this would force the British to retreat north away from Philadelphia and save the capital city from capture.

But Washington knew that the Americans were outnumbered. He decided to head north to Brandywine Creek instead. He thought this would be a better place to face the enemy. The Americans camped on the northern side of the creek. There were four places where the British might cross. Washington split his army to defend these **fords**. Washington sent Anthony to Chadd's Ford (about 25 miles southwest of Philadelphia) with the

In September 1777, George Washington moved his army to Philadelphia to protect the capital city from British forces. This map depicts an eastern view of the city.

Pennsylvania Line, a regiment from Virginia, and a group called Proctor's artillery. Washington believed that the British army would try to cross the Brandywine River here.

Britian's General Howe divided his army in two. Those commanded by General Knyphausen

During the battles of the Revolutionary War, American soldiers faced British soldiers, who were armed with bayonets, as shown here in this reenactment.

went to Chadd's Ford. Knyphausen was a Hessian soldier hired by the British to help fight the Continental Army. His job at Chadd's Ford was to keep the Americans busy. The rest of the army, under Howe and Lord Cornwallis, planned to circle around behind the Americans and attack from behind.

Washington ordered Anthony to charge across the creek and attack the British. Anthony had nearly defeated Knyphausen when he received a message. The message gave him wrong information about the position of the British army. There was some brief confusion, causing a pause in the action. The delay cost the Americans their chance for victory.

In the meantime, Cornwallis attacked the right side of the American army with 7,000 men. Knyphausen strengthened his attack at Chadd's Ford. Anthony held his position for more than three hours. But he finally ordered a retreat when he found out about Cornwallis' plan to attack him from behind. The Battle of Brandywine was a major defeat for the Americans.

On September 12, 1777, Washington moved his army to Philadelphia. The British traveled northwest, intending to cross the Schuylkill

River. Washington followed them. The two armies met on September 16. Anthony led the attack on Lord Cornwallis' troops. The fight had just started when a fierce rainstorm began. It rained for the next 24 hours and ruined the Americans' ammunition. Washington was forced to retreat north toward Pigeon Creek.

At the same time, Washington sent Anthony and about 1,500 men to attack the rear of the British army. He planned to slow them down by intercepting their baggage train. This would give Washington time to obtain fresh ammunition and arrive at the fords of the Schuylkill River before the British.

Anthony and his men camped between the Warren and Paoli taverns on September 18. The British were stationed to the northeast, about four miles away from the Americans. General William Smallwood, with 1,850 militia, was supposed to join Anthony.

The next morning, Anthony marched his troops close to the British camp, where he was surprised to see them still asleep. He did not attack. Anthony watched the British camp. It looked as though they would not start to move until after supper. Anthony believed the enemy did not know his position. He was wrong. A spy had given General Howe information about the number of men in Anthony's camp and its exact location.

Anthony received word that Howe planned to break camp at two o'clock in the morning. He ordered General Smallwood to bring the militia at once. Anthony planned to surprise the enemy and attack while the British were packing up their camp. He told his men to rest, but to lie on top of their ammunition to keep it dry.

Late that evening, Anthony's men brought a prisoner to him. Anthony recognized the man as one of his neighbors. He had come to warn them that the British knew their location and were planning to attack that night.

Brigadier General Wayne thought about his next move. He decided to let his men sleep, while waiting for General Smallwood. But he assigned extra guards to watch for the enemy. Smallwood did not arrive. The British approached the American camp very quietly. They attacked the guards with **bayonets**. No one was able to warn the sleeping soldiers. Finally, there was a scream, and the British were in the American camp.

Anthony shouted to Colonel Humpton to organize the men and march northwest to meet Smallwood. He had to repeat the order three times before Humpton obeyed. Humpton marched the men between the campfires, making them easy targets. The British attacked with bayonets. Sixty-three Americans were killed, and 70 were taken prisoner. The British only lost nine men–three killed and six wounded. This incident became known as the Paoli Massacre.

Anthony was blamed for the Paoli Massacre. Fellow officers accused him of not taking **precautions** to protect his men, especially after being warned of the attack. Anthony was very upset by this **criticism** and demanded his own court martial. Washington agreed. On October 24, a military court reached the conclusion that Anthony ". . . on the night of the 20th of September last, did every duty that could be expected from an active, brave and vigilant officer."

The morning after the Paoli Massacre, the British marched along the south side of the Schuylkill River. Washington kept up with

While the British led by General Grey were brutally attacking the Americans at Paoli, a special detachment was sent to Waynesborough. The soldiers surrounded the Wayne home. They thought they would find Anthony Wayne there. Anthony had become troublesome to the British and they wanted to get rid of him. The commander of the detachment was very polite to the ladies and treated them kindly. Nothing was taken from the house, and no damage was done. This behavior was unusual for the British in wartime.

them, marching the American army on the north side of the river. Howe appeared to be headed for Reading, Pennsylvania, an important American supply depot. On the night of September 22, Howe crossed the river unexpectedly. He camped at the village of Germantown. This move placed British troops between Washington's army and the city of Philadelphia, leaving the American capital open to attack.

Howe sent Cornwallis to capture Philadelphia and the nearby forts. He left a small British force at Germantown, and Washington thought about attacking. He asked the advice of his generals. Most were against it. But Wayne, Smallwood, Scott, and Porter wanted to attack without delay, and Washington agreed.

Between September 30 and October 3, the American army moved closer to the enemy. In preparing for the attack, Washington divided the army into four columns. One column would meet the British left **flank**. Another would cover the British right flank. General Sullivan and General Wayne would take their divisions to meet the center of the British line.

The Americans began to march on the night of October 3. By the next morning, they had arrived just north of the British post at Mount Airy. Men were sent to eliminate the enemy's

Benjamin Chew's house stood at the edge of German-town. General Knox and his troops wasted valuable time firing against these soldiers instead of assisting on the front line.

sentries. One of the guards was able to warn the British, and they began to retreat. Wayne and Sullivan chased them through Germantown. Six companies of British soldiers led by Colonel Musgrave took shelter inside Pennsylvania Chief Justice Benjamin Chew's house, which stood at the northern edge of the town.

Wayne and Sullivan chased Musgrave's regiment. Just past the house, they found themselves facing the main part of the British army. In the meantime, General Knox came to Chew's house, which was occupied by British soldiers. He stopped with two brigades and fired on the house for half an hour. This wasted valuable time because his soldiers were needed on the front line.

At the same time, Wayne and Sullivan made a large dent in the British defense. The British were retreating, and the Americans were close to victory. But it was extremely foggy that night, and an American brigade commanded by General Adam Stephen became confused in the fog. When the brigade saw some of Anthony's troops, they fired. The confusion spread through the entire American army. At this point, Washington had no choice but to retreat.

The British quickly took advantage of the situation, pushing the Americans back to White Marsh Church. Anthony covered the retreat as he had done in the Battle of Three Rivers and received wounds in his hand and foot. The Battle of Germantown was a defeat for the Americans. Washington moved his army to Valley Forge, Pennsylvania, for the winter.

The journey to Valley Forge was difficult; there was already snow on the ground. Nearly 12,000 men completed the march. By the time they arrived, almost 3,000 of them were barefoot or without proper clothing. Those who were able cut down trees to build log cabins. But the cabins had no floors, and wind blew through the spaces between the logs. There were no beds and very few blankets. The soldiers often had no meat or bread for many days.

Near the end of winter, Baron Friederich von Steuben arrived in Valley Forge. He was a Prussian soldier who had fought in the army of Frederick the Great. Von Steuben trained the soldiers, showing them how to use a bayonet and how to march in line. He also taught them how to work together in the battlefield. Von Steuben's training

Baron Friedrich von Steuben trained these Continental soldiers at Valley Forge on how to use a bayonet and work together in the battlefield.

would be very helpful to the Americans in the coming battles. Anthony paid close attention to von Steuben's lessons on how to use a bayonet.

On February 6, 1778, France and the United States signed a treaty. According to the agreement, France recognized America's Independence and promised to help fight the British. As a result, Britain declared war on France.

Fearing a French blockade of the Delaware River, the British army led by Sir Henry Clinton left Philadelphia by mid-June. The army marched into New Jersey on the way to New York. When General Washington learned that the British were moving, he followed them. He sent scouts to gather information. They told Washington that the British position in New Jersey was well-protected by woods and swamps. A successful attack would be difficult.

Washington ordered General Charles Lee to attack the British at dawn. He told Lee to send 700 men to watch the British during the night. If the enemy started to move, Lee's men had orders to fight and delay them as long as possible.

Lee did not send the men until daylight. By then, the enemy was already moving. When Washington found out, he ordered Lee to march immediately to catch the British. Anthony and

1,000 handpicked men marched with Lee. Soon, Lee got word that a group of 800 British soldiers were waiting near Monmouth Courthouse, New Jersey, to attack the Americans. He sent Anthony with 700 men to meet them. Anthony and his men fought so well, the British had to retreat and send for help.

In the meantime, soldiers from Lee's army stumbled into General Washington's camp. They told Washington that the Americans were close to victory. Washington didn't believe them until he heard it from his own scouts. Then, he charged forward and met Lee's army, which was retreating. Washington ordered them to turn around, and he sent them to help Anthony. He was angry with Lee and questioned him. Lee told Washington, "American soldiers can not fight British grenadiers." Washington shouted back, "They can fight any upon the face of the earth."

The British grenadiers were a group of men who were skilled in using the bayonet. These men were commanded by Colonel Monckton.

When Cornwallis arrived with the main British army, he ordered Monckton to charge. Anthony was ready. He waited until the grenadiers were only a few yards away. Then he gave the order to fire. The enemy was no match for the determined Americans. Colonel Monckton was one of the first killed, and his men eventually retreated.

In his report to Congress after the battle, Washington commended Anthony for "good conduct and bravery." Although the Americans claimed victory, neither army won the Battle of Monmouth.

Arthur St. Clair was promoted to major general in charge of the Pennsylvania Line. Anthony Wayne was angry because he thought that he should have gotten the promotion.

4

The War Turns

Once the French offered their help, the American people believed the war would end quickly. When Anthony Wayne again wrote to the authorities asking for clothing and blankets for his troops, his letter was ignored a second time. It bothered him that the ladies and gentlemen of Pennsylvania society had the finest clothes while his soldiers were freezing and had nothing to wear.

Anthony made a speech to the Pennsylvania Assembly. He begged them to help his soldiers. Finally, the assembly passed a law giving soldiers of the Pennsylvania Line half pay for life, new uniforms, and freedom from taxes on their land. It took a few months for the law to take effect. In the meantime, Anthony built log cabins, so the men would have shelter for the cold winter months ahead.

Anthony had been doing the work of a major general since he took command of the Pennsylvania Line. He trained his soldiers to be the best division in the American army. Despite his excellent service record, he was not promoted. Major General Arthur St. Clair was placed in charge of the Pennsylvania Line instead. St. Clair received the promotion because of his experience in the British army before the war.

Anthony felt hurt. He wrote a letter of **resignation** but decided not to send it. Instead, he asked for a leave from the army. It was granted, and he returned to Pennsylvania.

A short time later, Anthony wrote to Washington. He asked the general to put him in command of a corps of light infantry. Washington liked the suggestion, and in June, he sent for Anthony and began choosing men for the corps. The men came from every state. They were veterans of many battles with the British.

Sir Henry Clinton commanded the British troops in New York. In late May 1779, he sailed up the Hudson River with a large force of soldiers. On June 6 they captured two American forts. Soldiers from Stony Point were able to escape. Those from Verplanck's Point were taken prisoner.

The fort at Stony Point stood on a rocky cliff high above the river. It was surrounded by water on three sides. There was a swamp along the fourth side. At low tide, there was a sand bar across the swamp. The Americans had built a road through the swamp to allow passage in and out of the fort. Immediately after the take over, the British strengthened the fort's defenses. They placed cannons and other weapons along the walls. Stony Point was very strong.

On July 1, Anthony Wayne arrived at Washington's headquarters. Washington immediately sent him to Donderberg Mountain. From there, Anthony was able to see the defenses at Stony Point. Washington wanted to get Anthony's opinion about the possibility of storming the fort.

The fort was so well protected that Anthony advised against an attack. But Washington wanted to try. They decided that a nighttime assault would offer the best chance for victory.

Washington gave Anthony his plan for the attack on July 10. They

In July 1780 food supplies in the American camp were very low. Washington sent Anthony to gather cattle and grain. The British were also looking for food. Anthony's men clashed with them several times during the mission. At first, Anthony had trouble finding food. Then, he decided to steal cattle from the British. The Americans raided the British herds and brought the meat back to their troops.

British Major André wrote a poem about the event. "The Cow Chace" was published in the *Royal Gazette*. In it, André poked fun at Anthony and belittled the cause of the Americans.

were very careful to keep the details secret. They took every precaution not to make the enemy suspicious. Not even their own soldiers knew the arrangements.

On the morning of July 15, Anthony ordered the men to line up for inspection. Their weapons had to be in good working order. Exactly at noon, the men began to march west without speaking. When they reached the mountains, they rested. No one was allowed to leave the group. They continued their march until 8 o'clock at night. They were one and a half miles from Stony Point.

The men finally learned the purpose of their mission. They were going to recapture Stony Point. The first five men to enter the fort would be rewarded with money. Any man who tried to retreat would be shot. Anthony wasn't taking any chances. He was determined to be successful.

The light infantry consisted of three divisions. The one commanded by Colonel Febiger was to march to the southern end of the swamp, cross the sandbar, and charge up the south side of the fort. Anthony marched with this division. The second division was commanded by Colonel Butler. They would cross the sandbar on the north side of the fort and charge from there. The third division led by Major Murfree would march across the road toward the fort. At the sound of gunfire from the enemy, they would charge the fort and make the enemy think that Murfree was leading the main attack.

Each soldier was to wear a piece of white paper in his hat. This way the Americans would recognize their own troops, since they still did not have uniforms. At 11:30, Anthony gave the order to move out. When Anthony and Febiger reached the sandbar, it was underwater. The tide had come in, and the water was waist deep. They moved ahead anyway. A British guard caught sight of them and fired. Murfree's men heard the shots and charged the fort. As the British fired, 17 Americans were shot. Anthony was hit in the head by a musket ball, but it didn't stop him. He shouted to his men, "March on!"

It was a fierce battle. At last, the British threw down their weapons and surrendered. Sixty-three British had been killed, and 543 were taken prisoner. Only 15 Americans were killed and 83 were wounded. Anthony's scalp wound healed quickly.

The capture of Stony Point was a high point in Anthony's career. He had trained his men well. They lived up to the faith that he had in them. The battle proved to the American people that they could fight the British and win.

On July 26, 1779, Congress decided to thank Anthony Wayne in a special way. He was awarded a gold medal "for his brave, prudent and soldierly conduct in the spirited and well-conducted attack on Stony Point."

In late September 1780, British major John Andre was taken prisoner by three American soldiers. He was carrying plans for a British takeover of West Point in New York. American

**American General Benedict Arnold betrayed
the Continental Army in return for money and
a high rank in the British army.**

general Benedict Arnold was in command of the

fort. He offered to help the British in return for

money and a high rank in the British army.

Arnold was a **traitor,** who weakened the defenses at West Point by sending troops away on phony errands. When Washington found out, he sent for Anthony, who marched his brigade 16 miles in the middle of the night. They arrived at West Point and kept the fort from falling into British hands.

In December 1780, Anthony was in command of a brigade in the Pennsylvania Line. At the end of that month, the term of service for many of the soldiers was coming to an end. But Congress expected them to stay. The soldiers were tired of being cold and hungry. A group of 1,300 men left camp and marched toward Philadelphia. Anthony and some fellow officers followed them. When they reached the city, Anthony and the others talked to Congress. An agreement was finally reached. Those whose service had ended were paid and allowed to leave, and Congress, at last, supplied the troops with food and clothing. The men were grateful to Anthony.

That spring, Anthony traveled to Virginia with 800 men from the Pennsylvania Line. He reported to General Lafayette on June 7, 1781, at Fredericksburg. Lafayette had just learned that General Cornwallis was about to cross the James River at Green Spring on his way to Portsmouth, Virginia. Anthony and his men were ordered to spy on the British and attack their troops. But it was a trap. Instead of meeting only a small British force, Anthony found himself facing Cornwallis' entire army. He attacked anyway. Cornwallis was surprised that Anthony would attack with such a small force. He thought the rest of the American army must be near. He pulled back his troops, and Anthony was able to retreat.

Just before the **skirmish** at Green Spring, Anthony camped with his 800 men at York. A soldier called "Jemy the Rover" was with him. Jemy was a good soldier, but he often had too much to drink and misbehaved in camp. As a punishment, he was sent to the guardhouse. He asked the guard if Anthony was angry with him.

The Marquis de Lafayette, a French nobleman who believed in freedom, led a combined French and American army in Virginia.

The man replied that Anthony was mad. Jemy repeated the words, "Mad Anthony." From that day on he was known as "Mad Anthony Wayne." Other accounts say he earned the nickname for his love of danger.

British General Charles Cornwallis (right) is shown surrendering to General George Washington at Yorktown, Virginia, on October 19, 1781.

The final blow for the British army came on October 19, 1781 at Yorktown, Virginia. The Continental Army, aided by the French, surrounded Cornwallis and forced him to surrender.

During this action, Anthony was stationed between Portsmouth and Petersburg, Virginia. His assignment was to prevent Cornwallis from escaping into North Carolina.

In January 1782, Anthony went to Georgia. The British and Americans were still fighting there. The British force far outnumbered the Americans. Anthony established his headquarters at Ebenezer, 25 miles north of the city of Savannah. He built forts that stretched from Ebenezer southwest to the Ogeechee River. He planned to trap the British in Savannah and cut them off from their allies to the west.

The Creek Indians of Georgia were allies of the British. In February, Anthony heard that a large number of Creek chiefs were on their way to Savannah. Anthony's soldiers dressed in British uniforms and went to meet the chiefs. The fake British soldiers brought them to the American camp. Anthony spoke to them and asked them not to help the British. Soon after this meeting, the chiefs went home.

Anthony Wayne and his men fought the British in Savannah, Georgia, winning freedom from England for the state on July 11, 1782.

That May, Anthony got word that a group of British soldiers had left the city of Savannah to meet a band of Creek Indians. Anthony wanted to attack the British before they could join with the Creeks. He marched his small group of soldiers four miles at night through a dangerous swamp. When they reached the road on the other side of the swamp, the British were waiting for them. Anthony ordered his soldiers to attack. The British force outnumbered Anthony's by five to one, but Anthony's men attacked with tremendous strength, scattering the entire British force into the swamp.

The British finally gave up, leaving the city on July 11, 1782. The people of Georgia were grateful to Anthony for his help in freeing their state. The Georgia legislature even voted to buy a plantation for Anthony. That winter he spent time with the Creek and Cherokee Indians working out a peace treaty.

By June 1783, American soldiers were allowed to return home. They were officially discharged from the army in December. On October 10, 1783, Congress finally promoted Anthony to brevet major general.

On the night of June 24, 1782, at one o'clock in the morning, a band of Native Americans attacked Anthony's camp with the help of a British officer. The Indians captured two large field guns from Anthony's guards. The Americans, who had been sleeping, quickly awoke and began to fight. A chief, named Guristersijo, attacked Anthony. He struck back with his sword, fatally wounding the man. As the chief lay dying, he raised a gun and fired. The shot just missed Anthony but killed his horse. The other Indians then escaped.

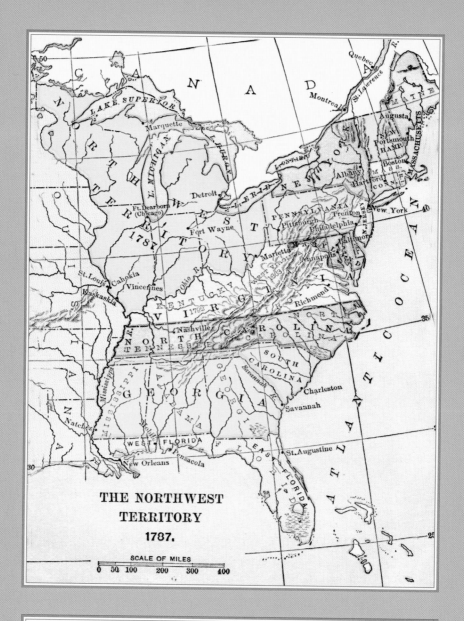

THE NORTHWEST
TERRITORY
1787.

SCALE OF MILES
0   50 100   200   300   400

This map shows the Northwest Territory in 1787. Congress passed the Northwest Ordinance that year. This created the process by which territories could become states. The ordinance also pledged good faith toward the Indians and their land.

War on the Frontier

Anthony Wayne retired from the army in 1783. He wanted to stay in Georgia and manage the rice plantation granted to him by the Georgia legislature, but he didn't have enough money to operate the farm. So Anthony eventually sold it and returned to Pennsylvania.

Anthony was elected to the Pennsylvania Assembly the following year. He worked to help his state recover from the war. In 1787, Anthony went to the Constitutional Convention, where he voted to ratify the new Constitution of the United States.

In 1791, Anthony was elected to represent Georgia

in the House of Representatives. Without his knowledge, the election had been arranged by some of his friends. After an investigation, Anthony lost his seat in the House.

In the meantime, Congress passed the Northwest Ordinance in 1787. Americans began to settle in the Northwest Territory. Native Americans believed white people were stealing their land and attacked the settlers. By 1790, about 1,500 settlers had been killed.

The British still occupied forts in the Northwest Territory. They had agreed to give them up at the end of the Revolutionary War, but they did not. The British encouraged the Indians to fight the Americans, hoping to weaken the new government.

The settlers begged the United States government for help. In 1790, General Josiah Harmer went to the Northwest Territory with Federal troops and militia. They attacked and burned Indian villages, making the Indians even angrier. On November 3, 1791, General St. Clair camped near the Wabash River with 1,400 soldiers. The

Indians attacked, and St. Clair was killed. Many of the soldiers lost their lives as well. It was a devastating defeat for the settlers.

President George Washington sent for Major General Anthony Wayne. He was a little unsure of his choice but wrote to a friend, "Wayne has many good points as an officer." In April 1792, Washington appointed Anthony commander in chief of the Legion of America.

At the same time, Washington tried to reach a peaceful settlement to the conflict. He sent Colonel John Hardin and Major Alexander Truman to talk to the Native Americans. After welcoming them, the Indians killed the men. Washington continued his efforts to negotiate for peace by sending three more agents to meet with the Indians in Detroit.

Anthony went to Pittsburgh to train his troops. Many of the men who were picked for the army were homeless men or criminals. Some, upon learning they were to fight the Native Americans, **deserted**. After gathering enough **recruits**, Anthony sent them to a camp named Legionville on the Ohio River. There, he trained his men during the winter of 1792–93.

In May the army moved to Fort Washington, near Cincinnati. Anthony worked with the men for two years, teaching them everything he knew about war. He drilled them every day, and taught them to use guns and bayonets. The troops were so well trained, that their reputation was known even among the Indians. The British officials in Detroit protested Anthony's work. They claimed it would hurt the peace talks.

That August, the peace negotiations broke down. By the time Anthony got the news, it was almost winter. It was too late to launch an attack. Anthony moved the army to Greenville, Ohio, and settled in for the winter. The fighting would have to wait until spring. Unfortunately, the delay also gave the British time to prepare the Indians to meet the Americans.

Chief Little Turtle went to Canada for help. He, along with the chiefs of other tribes, met with Lord Dorchester, a British nobleman. Dorchester led the Indians to believe the British were on their side. In the spring of 1794, Dorchester ordered British soldiers to build Fort Miami, near the Maumee Rapids in Ohio. The fort was very strong. It was built to withstand an assault by cannons. Any attempt to capture the fort would be disastrous to the attackers. The British also promised the Indians many soldiers to help fight the Americans.

After completing his work in the northwest, Anthony Wayne left Greenville and headed home to Pennsylvania. He arrived in Philadelphia on February 6, 1796. As he neared the city, an honor guard on horseback came out to greet him. Fifteen guns fired a salute as he crossed the river by ferry. The sound of bells announced his arrival. Thousands of Pennsylvanians lined the streets and greeted him with cheers and shouts of joy. There were fireworks demonstrations in the evening because the hero had finally come home.

Meanwhile, Anthony sent a group of soldiers from Greenville to the place where St. Clair had been defeated (now Indiana). He ordered them to build another fort, which he named Fort Recovery. On June 29, Indians attacked. Even though the American force was small, it was able to drive the enemy away.

In late July, General Charles Scott arrived

with troops from Kentucky. Anthony and Scott marched the army north but managed to fool the Indians into thinking they were headed in a different direction. Over the next few weeks, Anthony ordered his men to build several forts. The first was Fort Adams on the St. Marys River. Fort Defiance and Fort Deposit were next.

The next month, Anthony's scouts told him that Indians were waiting for the Americans at a place called Fallen Timbers (near what is now Toledo, Ohio). It had been named that because a tornado had hit, knocking over many trees. There were many hiding places from which the enemy could attack. The Indians were sure they would defeat the Americans. They expected soldiers from Fort Miami to arrive at any time. The fort was only two miles away. They had no reason to think that the British would not keep their promise to help.

On the morning of August 20, Anthony led a column of soldiers along the Maumee River. He was suffering from gout, a painful disease that affects the joints, and had to be helped onto his

American Indians are shown here in battle with the colonists over land in the Northwest Territory.

horse. After a short ride, the Americans saw the Indians and charged. Anthony ordered 900 men to charge the enemy with bayonets. Soldiers on horseback shot at the Indians, who began to run. The Americans continued their assault, chasing them into the woods. When the Indians got to the British fort, they found the gates closed. The British had no intention of helping them.

The Battle of Fallen Timbers was the last great

battle for control of the Northwest Territory. Anthony continued building forts after the war. Fort Industry was located in what is now Toledo, Ohio. A large fort was also built where the St. Marys and St. Joseph Rivers meet in Indiana. On October 20, 1794, Colonel John F. Hamtramck took command of this fort and named it Fort Wayne.

In November, Anthony arrived at Greenville. He spent the winter there working out a peace treaty with 15 tribes. In the agreement, the Indians gave a large amount of land to the Americans. In return, the tribes received almost $30,000 in goods and money. The Treaty of Greenville was signed on August 3, 1795. Anthony made sure the tribes understood everything in the agreement. As a result, the peace lasted a long time.

In the meantime, John Jay had gone to London to talk to the British. Jay tried to get them to pull their troops out of the American northwest. When British officials heard about Anthony's victory at Fallen Timbers, they signed the Jay Treaty, giving up their posts.

In July 1796, President Washington asked Anthony to travel again. The British were going to surrender their forts. Anthony was to take over these posts and man them with Americans. In November he left Detroit and headed for Presque Isle, Pennsylvania (now Erie).

The day before he arrived, he became ill with an attack of gout. The "Chief who never sleeps," as the Indians called him, died there on December 15, 1796. He was buried under the flagpole at the fort in Erie. It was his final wish "to lie under the shadow of the flag for which he had fought faithfully and well."

In 1809, "Mad" Anthony Wayne's son Isaac went to Presque Isle to bring his father's body home. He traveled in a small wagon. When the coffin was raised from the ground, it wouldn't fit in the carriage. Doctor James Wallace offered to help. He dissected the body, boiled it, and took the flesh off the bones. Anthony's flesh and clothing were returned to the grave at Presque Isle. Isaac took the bones home to be buried at St. David's churchyard in Radnor, near Philadelphia. According to legend, some of Anthony's bones fell out of the wagon on the trip home. Now, every New Year's Day, Mad Anthony's ghost travels the road looking for his bones.

GLOSSARY

allies–friends or associates, especially during wars.

bayonets–stabbing weapons attached to rifles.

convened–came together or assembled.

criticism–finding fault with someone or something.

deserted–abandoned.

flank–side of a body of troops.

fords–places where a river may be crossed by wading.

infantry–soldiers on foot.

militia–a group of civilian men called upon to serve in the military.

precautions–actions taken to protect against danger.

recruits–new members of a military force.

resignation–letter written to give up a job.

scholar–an educated student or pupil.

skirmish–small battle.

traitor–a person who betrays others.

CHRONOLOGY

1745 Born at Waynesborough in Chester County, Pennsylvania, on January 1.

1762 Attends Philadelphia Academy.

1763 Leaves Philadelphia Academy; opens own surveying office.

1764 Hired to survey land in Nova Scotia, Canada.

1766 Marries Mary Penrose on March 25.

1774 Inherits Waynesborough when father, Isaac, dies; sent to Philadelphia to represent Pennsylvania in the Second Continental Congress.

1776 Commissioned a colonel and given command of the Fourth Battalion of Pennsylvania.

1777 Promoted to brigadier general; participated in battles of Brandywine, Paoli, and Germantown; cleared of charges of neglect at court-martial.

1779 Leads the successful attack to recapture the fort at Stony Point, N.Y.

1783 Promoted to brevet major general; retires from the army.

1784 Elected to Pennsylvania Assembly.

1792 Appointed Commander in Chief of the Legion of America.

1794 Defeats the Miami Indians in the Battle of Fallen Timbers in the Ohio country.

1795 Negotiates the Treaty of Greenville.

1796 Dies at Presque Isle, Pennsylvania.

REVOLUTIONARY WAR TIME LINE ═══

1765 The Stamp Act is passed by the British. Violent protests against it break out in the colonies.

1766 Britain ends the Stamp Act.

1767 Britain passes a law that taxes glass, painter's lead, paper, and tea in the colonies.

1770 Five colonists are killed by British soldiers in the Boston Massacre.

1773 People are angry about the taxes on tea. They throw boxes of tea from ships in Boston harbor into the water. It ruins the tea. The event is called the Boston Tea Party.

1774 The British pass laws to punish Boston for the Boston Tea Party. They close Boston harbor. Leaders in the colonies meet to plan a response to these actions.

1775 The battles of Lexington and Concord begin the American Revolution.

1776 The Declaration of Independence is signed. France and Spain give money to help the Americans fight Britain. Nathan Hale is captured by the British. He is charged with being a spy and is executed.

1777 Leaders choose a flag for America. The American troops win some important battles over the British. General Washington and his troops spend a very cold, hungry winter in Valley Forge.

1778 France sends ships to help the Americans win the war. The British are forced to leave Philadelphia.

1779 French ships head back to France. The French support the Americans in other ways.

1780 Americans discover that Benedict Arnold is a traitor. He escapes to the British. Major battles take place in North and South Carolina.

1781 The British surrender at Yorktown.

1783 A peace treaty is signed in France. British troops leave New York.

1787 The U.S. Constitution is written. Delaware becomes the first state in the Union.

1789 George Washington becomes the first president. John Adams is vice president.

FURTHER READING

DeLeeuw, Adele. *Mad Anthony Wayne and the New Nation.*
Philadelphia, PA: Westminster Press, 1974.

January, Brendan. *The Revolutionary War.* New York: Children's
Press, 2000.

Stevenson, Augusta. *Anthony Wayne: Daring Boy.* Indianapolis,
IN: The Bobbs-Merrill Company, Inc., 1962.

Tucker, Glen. *Mad Anthony Wayne and the New Nation.* New York:
Grosset & Dunlap, 1953.

Wilson, Hazel. *The Story of Mad Anthony Wayne.* Harrisburg, PA:
Stackpole Books, 1973.

INDEX

PICTURE CREDITS

ABOUT THE AUTHOR

PATRICIA A. GRABOWSKI is an elementary school teacher and freelance writer. She has degrees in music and education. This is her sixth book. She lives in Staten Island, New York, with her husband and daughter.

Senior Consulting Editor **ARTHUR M. SCHLESINGER, JR.** is the leading American historian of our time. He won the Pulitzer Prize for his book *The Age of Jackson* (1945), and again for *A Thousand Days* (1965). This chronicle of the Kennedy Administration also won a National Book Award. He has written many other books, including a multi-volume series, *The Age of Roosevelt.* Professor Schlesinger is the Albert Schweitzer Professor of the Humanities at the City University of New York, and has been involved in several other Chelsea House projects, including the Colonial Leaders series of biographies on the most prominent figures of early American history.